The Beauty of
HISTORIC
ETHIOPIA

Camerapix Publishers International
NAIROBI

First published 1994 by
Camerapix Publishers International,
P. O. Box 45048,
Nairobi,
Kenya

© Camerapix 1994

Second impression 1997

This book was designed and produced by
Camerapix Publishers International,
P.O. Box 45048,
Nairobi,
Kenya

Edited by Brian Tetley and Jan Hemsing

ISBN 1 874041 18 0

Printed and bound in Singapore by Tien Wah Press Pte Ltd

*Half-title: Monks of the Ethiopian Orthodox Church, in a country where
Christianity has prevailed for 1600 years. Title page: Meadowland of
yellow daisies marks the September festival of Maskal — the season of
flowers — and commemorates the finding of the True Cross by St Helena,
wife of Constantine the Great. Contents page: Papyrus harvested from
Lake Tana is stacked on its shores. Pages 6-7: Ancient carved rock shrine
at Lalibela. Pages 8-9: The Blue Nile, born in Ethiopia's Lake Tana,
which covers 3,600 square kilometres, thunders over the Tissisat
('smoking water') Falls some kilometres downstream. Pages 10-11:
Musicians in the robes of the Ethiopian Orthodox Church celebrate
Timkat, the feast of Epiphany, Ethiopia's most celebrated and colourful
festival, at Lalibela.*

Contents

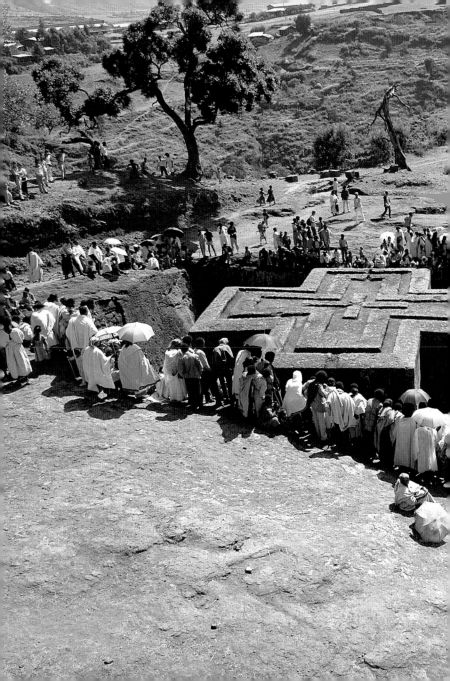

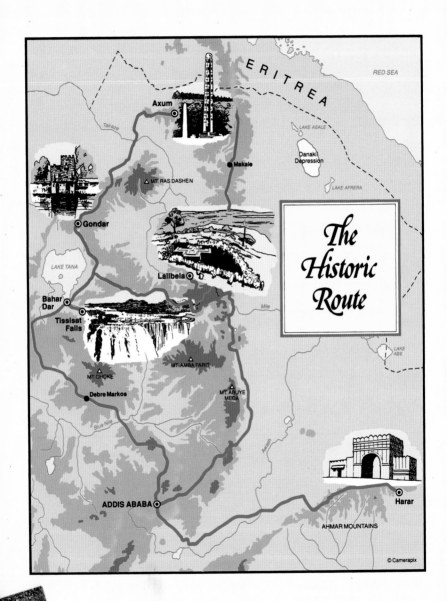

ERITREA

RED SEA

Axum

LAKE ASALE

Danakil
Depression

Makale

LAKE AFRERA

MT. RAS DASHEN

Tekeze

Gondar

The
Historic
Route

LAKE TANA

Lalibela

Mile

Bahar
Dar

LAKE
ABE

Tississat
Falls

MT. AMBA FARIT

MT CHOKE

MT. ABUYE
MEDA

Debre Markos

Blue Nile

Awash

Harar

ADDIS ABABA

AHMAR MOUNTAINS

© Camerapix

Above: The Grand Mosque at Harar with its two white-washed minarets dominate a broad courtyard. An important Muslim centre, Harar attracts pilgrims from all parts of the Islamic world.

Introduction

Welcome to the beauty of Ethiopia's Historic Route. The magnificent cultures and landscapes are indicative of an extraordinary past. It has left its mark on the land, the people and their monuments. Moreover, it is a past which began as the cradle of mankind.

Recent discoveries indicate that Ethiopia is the ancestral home in which *homo sapiens* took its first faltering footsteps away from the apes and towards its own unique identity. The cradle of mankind lies in the sere north-east of the country, close to the banks of the Awash River — where the Great Rift Valley forms a wide, low-lying triangle. There the fossilised remains of the oldest direct human ancestor, *Australopithecus afarensis*, dating back 3.5 million years — and thus at least a million years older than any previous hominid remains — were discovered. The initial find in 1974 took the form of an almost complete female skeleton. Nicknamed Lucy by palaeontologist Dr Donald Johanson, of the US Institute of Human Origins, this fossil is better known to Ethiopians as *Dinquinesh* — meaning 'thou art wonderful'.

Supplemented in the 1980s and 1990s by many other finds of similar antiquity along the Awash, and in the Omo River valley further south, *Dinquinesh* was an upright-walking hominid under four feet tall with a small brain and ape-like features. Her teeth, legs and pelvic bones, however, were distinctly human. The discovery pushed the horizon of mankind's ancestry back to a remote and unimaginably distant past.

Ethiopia also boasts some fine examples of Stone Age and pre-Stone Age cultures: flint tools have been found in river beds, and delicate paintings — almost half-a-million years old — on the walls of caves. The country was also one of the

earliest to make use of fire and crop cultivation. Later, the movement and interactions of peoples from the Horn of Africa and Southern Arabia created the country's first high civilisation — in the highlands overlooking the Red Sea coast.

Today's inhabitants of this region speak a Semitic language, Tigrinya, closely related to *Ge'ez*, the ancient tongue of Ethiopia still used in the liturgy of the Orthodox Church. Amharic, the *lingua franca* of modern Ethiopia, is another descendant of classical *Ge'ez*.

Together, the Amhara and Tigray peoples constitute the group long known to the outside world as Abyssinians — an epithet almost certainly derived from *Habashat*, the name of a South Arabian tribe that long ago migrated to the Horn of Africa. The idea that the *Habashat*, together with other nomadic Arab groups, were the progenitors of Ethiopia's highland civilisation, is strengthened by the fact that *Ge'ez* was linked to Sabaean, one of the original languages of South Arabia and hence, also, to Hebrew and to Arabic.

Such links, together with archaeological evidence, have conditioned research to the entire region. Perhaps inevitably, Ethiopia is seen by many as little more than an African outpost of an essentially Asiatic Semitic culture. This ignores, however, the effect of the other main ethnic component of Ethiopia and of the Horn of Africa as a whole — the Agaw, the Somali and the Oromo, who speak Hamitic, also sometimes referred to as Cushitic, languages and whose cultural contribution has also been immense.

New findings suggest that both the Semitic and Hamitic language families may derive from a single ancestral tongue, Hamito-Semitic, which originated in the eastern Sahara — before it became a desert — and not Asia.

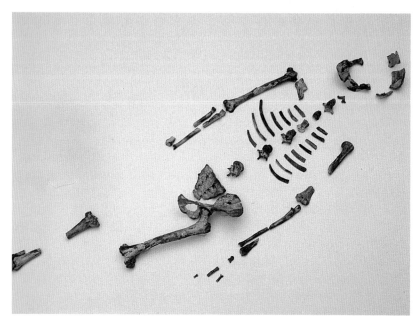

Above: The fossilised remains of
Australopithecus afarensis —
nicknamed "Lucy" — the oldest
direct human ancestor.

Right: Hand skeletons, reconstructed
with a mix of Afar fossil and modern
human bones show the human
characteristic of the
Australopithecus afarensis hand.

Opposite: The upper and lower jaws
of the Australopithecus afarensis,
with chimp skull above, and human
skull below, demonstrates the
intermediate evolutionary status of
the species.

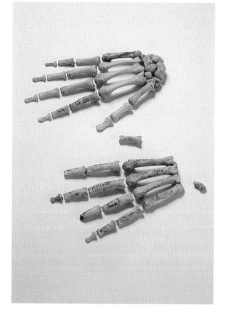

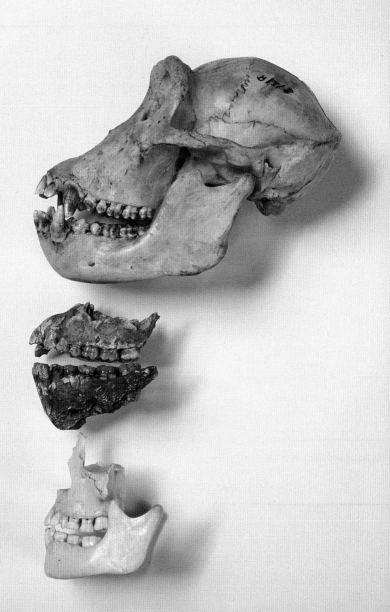

Curiously corroborated in certain respects by the Old Testament, this view suggests that climatic changes in ancient times prompted a migration across the Red Sea out of Africa and that the Semitic peoples of the Middle East — notably the Jews and the Arabs — owe their origins to this primordial exodus. Other speakers of the Hamito-Semitic tongue, however, moved southwards to colonise the Horn. There, possibly because of the divided nature of the region's dramatic landscapes, increasing linguistic and cultural specialisation led to the emergence of distinct ethnic groups.

Throughout many thousands of years, the tribes on the Arabian peninsula and those who stayed in Africa maintained some contact, with substantial movements perhaps in both directions. Thus, South Arabians such as the Habashat may well have been returning to an already established Semitic homeland.

Recorded histories in which Ethiopia is mentioned date back more than 4,000 years. The earliest records were compiled by two ancient centres of human civilisation, Persia and Egypt — both of which saw the Horn of Africa as an emporium of much-prized tropical products. Egyptian hieroglyphic inscriptions indicate that the Pharaohs obtained frankincense and myrrh from Ethiopia as long ago as 3,000 years before the birth of Christ. Trade with India also began in remote antiquity — the Horn has supplied the subcontinent with vast quantities of ivory from time immemorial.

Ancient contacts such as these nurtured and strengthened the emerging Semitic culture of northern Ethiopia, creating a kingdom that dominated the vital crossroads of Africa and Asia for almost a thousand years. Conducting its foreign trade through the Red Sea port of Adulis, the kingdom's capital was

Axum — described by Nonnosus, Ambassador of the Roman Emperor Justinian, as the greatest city of all Ethiopia.

Founded around 100 BC, Axum was itself descended from an even more ancient city-state — nearby Yeha, whose fabulous ruins still stand. Little of substance is known about Yeha, however. It was the Axumites who detailed the first civilisation of historic Ethiopia. The Axumites introduced a written language, *Ge'ez*, and created a new imperial power and political cohesion. They also gave Ethiopia a new religion — Christianity, in the fourth century AD. Their sophisticated and prosperous culture mobilised large groups of labour and enough wealth to build great edifices — monumental architecture that survives to the present day. These massive buildings and towering stone sculptures are eloquent witness to a high level of artistic ability and advanced engineering and mathematical skills.

The Axumites adopted Christianity in Ethiopia when much of the known world was immersed in paganism. The new religion gave birth to a rich ecclesiastical tradition — still vividly alive — and endowed the emerging nation with a unique sense of destiny. At the heart of this dynamic culture lies the legend of King Solomon and the Queen of Sheba — a biblical tradition that inspired a curious and important Ethiopic appraisal (first written down, from much earlier oral sources, in medieval times). This revised history made Axum the birthplace of the Queen of Sheba and anchored the Ethiopian people, and Ethiopian highland culture, firmly in the Old Testament. It claimed the son of Solomon and Sheba as founder of the Solomonic dynasty which came to an end in 1974 when the Emperor Haile Selassie was overthrown. It also depicted ruler and people as true descendants of the House of

19

Above: Modern stone-house at Axum, where the Ark of the Covenant is supposed to be preserved.

Above: Mysterious obelisks at Axum. No one knows the origins of these ancient stelae which have survived the centuries.

David. When the teachings of the New Testament were added to this, it became the blueprint of a Christian society remarkable for its creativity and its tolerance of the other great monotheistic faiths which coexist in Ethiopia — Islam and Judaism.

Manifestations of this vibrant religious energy date from the medieval period. The imposing monolithic churches of Lalibela, for example, built in the late twelfth and early thirteenth centuries, are ranked by UNESCO among the wonders of world heritage. In fact, they were not built at all in the conventional sense but physically sculpted from the living bedrock of the mountains in which they stand — in the region known as Wollo, which lies far to the south and east of Axum. Exquisitely carved on the outside, they house rare and beautiful murals and paintings within. Furthermore, they are superb examples of the benefits that accrue to a culture from a combination of political power and religious inspiration. These remarkable buildings are the concept of a single monarch, Lalibela, who ruled from AD 1185 to 1210 and who seems to have been determined to build for his people a new Jerusalem in the highlands of Ethiopia.

From the thirteenth to the sixteenth centuries, despite frequent wars and invasions, intellectual culture continued to flourish in this ancient land with the establishment of many monasteries, notably on the secluded islands of Lake Tana, with the writing of successive royal chronicles — invaluable to scholars for the accurate historical records that they contain — the translation of further biblical and other texts into into *Ge'ez*, and the production of many superb illuminated manuscripts. Imperial splendour grew in tandem with these developments and eventually gravitated to the beautiful fortress city of

Gondar — which lies just north of Lake Tana and was established as the capital in 1636 by Emperor Fasilidas. Gondar is rightly renowned for its many fairy-tale castles, palaces and beautiful churches built not only by Fasilidas himself but also by his equally illustrious successors: Yohannes I, Iyasu the Great, Bakaffa and others.

At the same time, Ethiopia's mercantile Islamic culture rose up side by side with that of the Christians. The town of Harar, in the east of the country, is a fine example of this alternative strand of Ethiopia's broad and diverse heritage and occupies a proud place of its own along the historic route that so many now set out to explore.

Above: Ornate design in the interior of one of Lalibela's rock-hewn churches.

Opposite: One of the rock-hewn marvels of Lalibela.

1. Yeha, Axum, Debra Damo

Ethiopia's historic route begins with a glance at the tantalising remains of Yeha — the country's earliest high civilisation.

In a remote part of Tigray region, Yeha lies several hours drive from the more accessible city of Axum. The journey takes you on rough tracks through dramatic highland scenery and eventually ends in a beautiful and serene agricultural hamlet. It is there, close to a much more recent Christian church, that you may see the towering ruins of Yeha's Temple of the Moon — built more than 2,500 years ago, in Sabaean times.

The temple is an imposing rectangular edifice. Though it has long since lost its roof and upper storeys the ruins stand some twelve metres in height. As evening falls, the temple's finely dressed and polished limestone reflects the glow of the setting sun with a warmth and brilliance that cannot be accidental. The huge, precisely fitted blocks from which the inward-inclining walls are formed seem to bear out ancient opinion that Sabaean buildings could be filled with water without a single drop being lost.

Apart from the temple, however — which speaks eloquently of the works of a high civilisation — little or nothing is known about the people who built this great edifice. Indeed, their origins are wrapped in mystery of which, perhaps, the greatest is this: if a culture had evolved to the level of sophistication required to build monuments of such quality in the highlands of Tigray by the sixth century BC, then what were its antecedents? What came before it? And how far back does Ethiopian civilisation really go? So far the archaeologists have uncovered no convincing answers to these questions.

Founded perhaps 500 years after the decline of Yeha, much more is known about the historic highland city of Axum —

together with its Red Sea port, Adulis. The latter was abandoned suddenly — probably in the sixth century AD — as the result of an invasion from Arabia, and was never resettled. On the other hand, protected by the mountains of northern Tigray, Axum survives to exert a profound influence on the imaginations and spiritual lives of many Ethiopians.

A small and lowly town surrounded by dry hills, modern Axum does not easily yield evidence of the splendours and pageantry of its glorious past. Its drab breeze-block houses, roofed with corrugated iron, look little different from those of any other contemporary highland settlement and its people seem remarkable only for their impassive stoicism. Part buried, however, but also part exposed, the extensive traces of noble buildings with large stone foundations are found there side by side with the ruins of even more impressive structures: temples, fortresses, and rich palaces. Adding substance to ancient legends of fire-breathing monsters and testifying to the lost truths embedded in myths and fables, the bones of bygone eras protrude everywhere through the soil. Even today, long-buried hordes of gold, silver and bronze coins are exposed by heavy downpours of rain.

Axum, historians like Richard Pankhurst tell us, was a great commercial civilisation trading with distant lands, among them Egypt, Arabia, Persia, India and Ceylon. To countries such as these the ancient Axumites exported gold, ivory, rhinoceros-horn, hippopotamus hide and slaves, and imported all kinds of textiles — cottons and silks, as well as knives, swords and drinking cups, metal for local manufacture into all sorts of objects, and numerous luxury goods, including gold and silver plate, military cloaks for the nobility, olive oil and lacquerware.

Above: Ruins of an ancient temple at Yeha in the mountains of Ethiopia.

Opposite top: Mellow stone of Yeha shrine has survived more that 1,000 years.
Opposite: Detail of the stonework in the pre-Christian temple at Yeha.

29

Testimony to the importance of this trade is to be seen in the Axumite currency, in gold, silver and bronze, which was inscribed either in Greek or Ge'ez, and issued for several hundred years by over twenty different Axumite kings. Most of this fascinating money was struck in the city, but other coins were probably minted at Adulis, as well as in South Arabia, part of which in the sixth century was under Axumite control.

The Axumites of old were also renowned as fine builders and craftsmen, skilled in particular as masons and metal workers as will be evident to anyone visiting the city's antiquities, and especially in its small, but well worth visiting museum.

Axum's greatest significance, however, is as the epicentre of the Queen of Sheba dynasty, upon which rests the notion of the sacred kingship of the Semitic peoples of Ethiopia — a notion that links the recent past to ancient times in most unambiguous fashion. The 1955 Constitution introduced by the late Emperor Haile Selassie, for example, only reiterated what everybody then regarded as incontrovertible truth. It stated: "The Imperial Dignity shall remain perpetually attached to the line of Haile Selassie I, whose Line descends without interruption from the dynasty of Menelik I, son of the Queen of Ethiopia, the Queen of Sheba, and King Solomon of Jerusalem. . . . By virtue of His Imperial Blood, as well as by the annointing which He has received, the Person of the Emperor is sacred, His Dignity inviolable and His Power indisputable. . . ."

Haile Selassie claimed to be the 225th monarch of the Solomonic line. His removal from power by junior army officers in 1974, and his death in obscure circumstances a year later, thus marked the end of an era — and the beginning of the end of an entire way of life.

The appeal to historical continuity is somewhat overstated in the 1955 Constitution. In fact, there were a number of interruptions to the rule of the Solomonic line — by no means the least important of which was the Zagwe dynasty which bequeathed to Ethiopia the priceless legacy of the Lalibela churches. Only late in the thirteenth century — after the intervention of a saint, Tekla Haimanot — was one of King Lalibela's successors persuaded to abdicate in favour of a candidate claiming Solomonic descent. That they should have abdicated at all, however, bears witness to the enduring mystique of the Solomon and Sheba legend.

Indeed, the power of this legend is such that it has infiltrated numerous cultures outside Ethiopia. The earliest written form still extant is preserved in two books of the Old Testament. These narrate that the Queen of Sheba, lured by Solomon's fame, journeyed to Jerusalem with a great caravan of costly presents and there communed with him of all that was in her heart. King Solomon, for his part, gave to the Queen of Sheba all her desire. . . . So she turned and went to her own land, she and her servants.

The Talmud also contains oblique references to the story, as does the New Testament in which Sheba is referred to as the Queen of the South. In addition, there is a fairly detailed account in the Qur'an, echoed in several Arabic and Persian folk tales of later date, in which she is known as *Bilgis*. Further afield, in southern Africa, the enigmatic stone ruins of Great Zimbabwe are said by some to have been the palace of the Queen of Sheba, and tribal elders still repeat their own fully evolved version of the legend.

Among all these different narratives, the Ethiopian legend — where Sheba's name becomes *Makeda* — is the richest and the most convincing, despite the fact that it does not seem to have been written down until medieval times. It appears in the Glory of Kings (the *Kebra Negast*), the Ethiopian national saga written in the fourteenth century.

The veneration of the Queen of Sheba as the spiritual ancestress of the Ethiopian people began much earlier, however. Indeed, the cult of *Makeda* may substantially predate the Christian era.

As set out in the *Kebra Negast*, the story is romantic and inspiring. The Queen of Sheba's capital city, *Debra Makeda*, is usually thought to refer to Axum. From there, it is said, she was persuaded to travel to the court of Solomon by a certain Tamrin — the head of her caravans — who had become much impressed by the King's wisdom and might. In Jerusalem a banquet of specially seasoned meat was given in her honour and, at the end of the evening, Solomon invited her to spend the night in his chambers. *Makeda* agreed but first extracted a commitment from the King that he would not take her by force. To this he assented, on the single condition that the Queen make a promise not to take anything in his house. Solomon then mounted his bed on one side of the chamber and had the Queen's bed prepared at the other side, placing near it a bowl of water. Made thirsty by the seasoned food she had consumed, *Makeda* soon awoke, arose, and drank the water. At this point Solomon seized her hand, accused her of having broken her oath and then worked his will with her.

That night the King dreamt that a great light of brilliance, the *shekina*, the divine presence, had left Israel and moved to Ethiopia. Shortly afterwards the Queen departed and returned

to her country and there, nine months and five days later, she gave birth to a son [Menelik, the founder of the Ethiopian Solomonic dynasty]. When the boy had grown up he went to visit his father who received him with great honour and splendour. After some time at Solomon's court, the youth determined to return once more to his mother's realm. Thereupon the King assembled the elders of Israel and commanded them to send their first-born sons with Menelik. Before the young men departed they abducted the Ark of the Covenant and took it with them to Ethiopia, which now became the second Zion.

Today a replica or symbol of the Ark of the Covenant, known as the *tabot*, occupies pride of place in the holy of holies of every Ethiopian Orthodox Church. These replicas — which derive their sanctity from their relationship to the true and original Ark still believed by Ethiopians to be kept at Axum — are so important that no church is considered consecrated without one.

Ethiopia's claim to the lost Ark of the Covenant is a vexed and contentious one. Many do believe this priceless Old Testament treasure rests in Axum, exactly where the Ethiopians say it is. It seems likely, however, that the Ark arrived in Ethiopia in the late fifth century BC, about 500 years after the time of Solomon, Sheba and Menelik, for completely different reasons from those set out in the national epic. There is some evidence that it was first installed on an island in Lake Tana where it remained for 800 years before finally being removed to Axum around the time of Ethiopia's conversion to Christianity in the fourth century AD.

The building where the Ark is said to lie is a small, unpretentious sanctuary built in 1965 on the orders of Haile

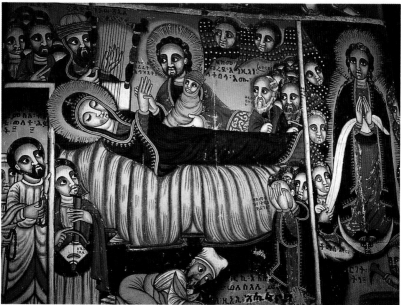

Above: Queen of Sheba's tomb and the ancient ruins of her palace at Axum.

Opposite top: The 400-year-old Church of St Mary of Zion at Axum was raised on the foundations of the fourth-century church of the same name that once stood there.
Opposite: Brilliant frescoes adorn the interior of Axum's Church of St Mary of Zion.

Selassie. The chapel, fashioned out of blocks of grey granite, stands at the heart of Axum's extensive monastic complex and is annexed to the seventeenth-century Cathedral of St Mary of Zion where the sacred relic previously rested. In line with a time-honoured tradition, only one man is allowed to set eyes upon the Ark itself: an elderly, especially holy monk who is charged with its care and preservation. The present custodian, Abba Tesfa Mariam, inherited the honour — and the burden — of guarding the Ark from a long line of previous monks stretching back into the mists of history. When a custodian is dying, according to tradition he must nominate his own successor with his last words.

The Church of St Mary of Zion was built around 1635 by Emperor Fasilidas — undoubtedly one of Ethiopia's greatest rulers. Still a place of active worship, it is notable for its crenellated, fortress-like walls. Its hushed interior, resplendent with many beautiful murals and paintings, evokes a mood of contemplation in an atmosphere of immense antiquity. This may have something to do with the fact that many of the stone blocks from which it is built predate the seventeenth century. They come from an extensive ruin that stands nearby. Only the ruins of its deeply entrenched foundations remain — all that is left of the original St Mary of Zion, built in the fourth century at the time of the conversion of the Axumite kingdom to Christianity. Twelve hundred years later, in the middle of the sixteenth century, it was razed by a fanatical Muslim invader, Ahmed Gragn — The Left Handed — whose forces swept across the Horn of Africa from Harar in the east and, at one time, threatened the complete extinction of Ethiopian Christendom.

By far the oldest church in Africa south of the Sahara, the

first St Mary's — as it is still referred to in Axum — was described some years before its destruction by the Portuguese friar Francisco Alvarez: "In this town [Axum], we found a noble church; it is very large, and has five naves of a good width and of a great length, vaulted above, and all the vaults are covered up, and the ceiling and sides are all painted; it also has a choir after our fashion. This church has a very large circuit, paved with flagstones, like gravestones, and it has also a large enclosure, and is surrounded by another large enclosure like the wall of a large town or city. . . ."

From Alvarez' account, it is apparent that the first St Mary of Zion church was a great five-aisled basilica. Aspects of its design are thought to have been borrowed from earlier, pre-Christian places of worship in Axum. In turn, these were later incorporated into the nearby clifftop monastery of Debra Damo — built in the sixth century and still standing. Experts believe St Mary's also served as the model for Beta Medhane Alem — the most extensive and ambitious of the twelfth-century monoliths in far-off Lalibela. They also believe it inspired another of the spectacular rock-hewn churches of that area — Beta Ghenetta Mariam — which stands in mountainous countryside some kilometres from Lalibela. In such fashion, despite the ravages of both time and man, do themes and patterns repeat themselves endlessly in Ethiopia. Perennial meanings are frequently disguised behind changing facades but nothing, it seems, is ever entirely lost.

Most enduring of all is the manner in which devout aspirations are embodied in architecture — buildings and monuments which transform into mystic and occult symbols for prayer. This tradition has an ancient pedigree in the Ethiopian highlands that began before the Christian era. Many

Above: Carved and raised thousands of years ago, time has taken its toll of many stelae at Axum which now lie fallen and broken.

Opposite: Lone shepherd boy stands in silhouette in the shadows of one of Axum's giant free-standing stelae.

of the oldest relics of Axum suggest an idolatrous veneration of celestial deities. The most notable, carved from single pieces of solid granite, take the form of towering obelisks. Several are more than 500 tonnes in weight and stand twenty metres high. The tallest — now a tumbled, fractured ruin — once reared more than thirty-three metres into the sky.

They seem less like prayers of stone and more like lightning-rods to heaven. The purpose of these prodigious monolithic stelae may have been to draw down power from the firmament in a ritual undoubtedly accompanied by occasional sacrifices. Most of the obelisks have altars at their bases, all aligned towards the rising sun. Four deep holes in the centre of one were presumably to collect blood from the sacrifices. Another smaller altar is dominated by a raised platform out of which has been chiselled a vessel resembling a chalice — again, no doubt, to receive the blood of the slaughtered victim. Channels have been cut at two of the platform's four corners to enable the blood to drain into the lower level, where three more vessels have been engraved. There is a complete series of smaller holes all round with two more channels at the corners to allow life's crimson ebb to flow to the ground.

The tallest stele still standing is just over twenty-three metres tall. Like many other monolithic Ethiopian works, of whatever era, it is carved to resemble a conventional building — in this case a nine-storey tower-house. The main decoration on the front is the depiction of windows and timber-beams. The space between each level is depicted by rows of symbolic log-ends. The house-like illusion is enhanced by the presence of a false door just above the altar at the bottom of the monument. Another feature — echoed, incidentally, in the

alternately recessed and projecting courses of Beta Ammanuel at Lalibela — is a shallow central alcove which rises from the base to the summit.

The motifs on the face are carried through on either side. The rear is completely plain, however, but for one circle in relief near the apex. At its centre is a representation of four spheres grouped together, with a fifth sphere touching the group's outer edge. The top of the stele is carved into a semi-circular form, symbolising the heavens. Scholars believe a metal plate with an image of the sun, engraved inside a crescent moon, was affixed to the front of this.

Of the fifty or so stelae in and around Axum, some are obviously early prototypes — crudely worked slabs of granite similar to Stonehenge in south-west England. One group of these undecorated prehistoric monuments stands on the Gondar road, about a kilometre outside Axum, close to the remains of a massive building with finely-mortared stone walls, deep foundations and an impressive throne room — said to be the Queen of Sheba's palace. Elsewhere there are stelae that seem to belong to an intermediate period: one about five metres high, for example, which is divided into storeys by four bands overlaid with symbolic rows of beam-ends.

The British archaeologist Theodore Bent observed in 1893 after a visit to Axum that: "We seem to have before us a highly perfected form of stone worship, associated with sacrifices to the sun and affording us a complete series, from the early rude monument to the exquisitely decorated monolith, leading up in architectural symbolism to the home of the great God above."

Another fallen Axum stele, almost nine metres long, bears a relief carving near its apex with a capital formed of two leaves

Above: Two of the old royal crowns preserved.

Opposite: Precious bronze cross, a sacred relic held in keeping at Axum's Church of St Mary of Zion.

supporting a square within a square surmounted by a triangle. This may be the earliest-ever representation of the Ark of the Covenant in Ethiopian art. It would have been carved onto the stele after the Ark was brought to Axum in the fourth century AD.

Yet another of Axum's famous obelisks, the second largest, can be seen in Rome, where it was taken in 1937 on the personal orders of Benito Mussolini. It has thus far not been returned, despite many Ethiopian requests for its restitution.

The last few centuries of the pre-Christian era in Axum were most probably characterised by a rich mix of exotic Judaic and indigenous pagan traditions. The former was brought by immigrants from South Arabia where Hebraic-Jewish admixtures had long been part of the civilisation while the latter drew its continuing power from deep within the Ethiopian hinterland. This mix may have been influenced by Roman and Greek cults such as Mithraism which made sacrifices to the sun god.

The Axumites were certainly in close contact with Greek culture for a long time. Around the fourth century AD the anonymous author of *The Periplus of the Erythrean Sea* described the ruler of Axum as a prince superior to most and educated with a knowledge of Greek. Third-century coins found at Axum, bearing pagan crescent-and-disc symbols identical to those atop some of the stelae, are inscribed in Greek. Similarly, a more extensive Greek inscription, from the early fourth century, still legible, has been found carved into a pillar of stone set up at Axum on the order of King Ezana to commemorate his victory over rebellious tribes. It touches Greek theology by giving thanks to Ares, "who is my father". Other sides of the stone are inscribed in Sabaean and *Ge'ez*.

King Ezana occupies a vital place in Ethiopian history. Near the end of his reign the Axumite realm converted to Christianity. The story, which is rooted in the rule of Ezana's father, King Ella Amida, is told by the fourth-century Byzantine theologian, Rufinius. He records that Meropius, a Christian merchant he describes as a philosopher of Tyre, once sailed to India with two Syrian boys, Frumentius and the younger Aedesius. Returning through the Red Sea their ship was seized and Meropius was killed. The boys survived, however, and were taken to King Ella Amida of Axum, who promptly made Aedesius his cup-bearer and Frumentius his treasurer and secretary.

The two boys were held in great affection by the King. But he died shortly afterwards leaving his infant son, Ezana, as his heir. Before his death, however, Ella Amida gave the two Syrians their freedom. With tears in her eyes, the Queen begged them to stay until Ezana came of age. In particular, she needed the help of Frumentius for, though loyal and honest, Aedesius was simple.

In the years that followed, the influence of Frumentius in the Axumite kingdom grew. He sought out foreign traders who were Christians and provided them with whatever was needed, supplying sites for buildings and in every way promoting the growth of the seed of Christianity in the country.

When Ezana ascended the throne, Aedesius returned to Tyre and Frumentius travelled to Alexandria, then a great centre of Christianity, to tell Patriarch Athanasius of the Christian work so far accomplished in Ethiopia. He begged the ecclesiastical leader to look for some worthy man to send as bishop over the many Christians already congregated. But

after considering all that Frumentius had said, Athanasius took him before a council of priests and declared: What other man shall we find in whom the spirit of God is as in thee who can accomplish these things? Athanasius then consecrated Frumentius and sent him back to Axum as Ethiopia's first Christian bishop.

Eventually, Frumentius's missionary endeavours were rewarded by the conversion of the King himself. Coins from Ezana's reign record the transition. Earlier ones bear a pagan crescent-and-disk but later examples are stamped uncompromisingly with the cross — in fact, they were among the earliest coins of any country to carry the Christian symbol.

The new religion spread rapidly. Two sixth-century kings, Kaleb and his son Gebre-Maskal, were great proclaimers of the faith: their catacombs lie deep beneath the ruins of a vast fortress on a hilltop overlooking Axum. The fortress was described in glowing terms by a contemporary visitor, Cosmas Indicopleustes, as the four-towered palace of the King of Ethiopia. The Graeco-Egyptian traveller also reported that everywhere there were churches of the Christians in which the gospel was being proclaimed.

This apparent golden age did not last. Towards the end of the sixth century the Axumite port of Adulis was sacked. Barely a hundred years later, Muslim invaders from Arabia seized and occupied much of the coastal zone. Deprived of its access to the sea, Axum swiftly sank into cultural and military decay.

Subject tribes like the Hamitic *Beja* — warlike nomads whose descendants still live in Eritrea and the neighbouring Red Sea hills of the Sudan — began a series of revolts in the northern provinces of the kingdom during the eighth and

ninth centuries. These rebellions were followed by an Agaw uprising in the west and south. The majority of the Agaw, who were pagan, were rallied by a formidable queen called Gudit (Judith). Historians are uncertain whether she was a worshipper of the sun and the moon or whether she adhered to a form of Judaism. All that is sure is that in the tenth century she attacked Axum, destroyed much of the ancient city, overthrew its last king, killed the royal princes — thus interrupting the Solomonic line — and tried to uproot the Christian faith.

In folklore, Queen Gudit is remembered as a monster and a destroyer of churches and as a result, women are still not allowed to enter many churches. The Queen, however, is also regarded by some as a champion of the Hamitic, or Cushitic, people of the highlands. She brought an end to centuries of domination by the Semitic overlords of Axum. The subsequent shift of secular power southwards from Tigray into Wollo, as one authority has it, was a necessary step in the integration of Abyssinia . . . . The Agaw people, hitherto subject to a Semitic or Semitised aristocracy, now gained the upper hand, and the distinctions of descent or class between rulers and ruled began to disappear.

The break with the Church which Gudit brought about was not nearly as violent as it seemed at the time. Indeed, by the twelfth century, large sections of the Agaw had converted passionately to Christianity. Under King Lalibela, they carved their prayers in stone with a devotion that survives with undimmed grandeur.

Some four hours drive from Axum — plus a further two hours stiff uphill walk from the point where the road ends — lies the spectacular monastery of Debra Damo, situated on an

Above: Panoramic view from the clifftop at Debra Damo.

Opposite: Visitors make the tricky rope ascent to the monastery of Debra Damo.

isolated clifftop in one of the wildest parts of Tigray.

Damo is unique and unforgettable although, as with most Ethiopian monasteries, women are not allowed to enter it. Even so, there is a daunting obstacle to the monastery: the only means of access is a climb of twenty-five metres up a sheer cliff. Monks lower a safety rope which visitors tie around their waists. Then they use a second, thicker rope to climb with. Some may reflect, as they make their way to the top, that because of this arduous, dangerous ascent the art treasures of Debra Damo have remained intact through the monastery's 1,400 tumultuous years of history.

The treasures include an extensive collection of illuminated manuscripts — among them the oldest surviving fragments of texts anywhere in Ethiopia — and intricate carvings on the beams and ceiling of the ancient church around which the monastery is built. There are no murals as such, but a large number of paintings are preserved there including several that depict the legend of the foundation of Debra Damo by Abuna Aragawi. He is a Saint who is believed to have been lifted onto the clifftop by a giant serpent. According to the legend expressed in a number of the paintings, the Archangel Gabriel stood by with a sword ready to slay the snake if it attacked Abuna Aragawi. It did not, however, and wrapped in its coils the Saint reached the top safely, dropping his cross on a stone which is today kissed by all who enter the monastery.

The bluff on which Damo stands is a real-life Shangri-La. Remote and beautiful, far from the hustle and bustle of the late twentieth century, the cool celestial island of rock offers panoramic views over the surrounding countryside and complete seclusion and peace for the hundred or so monks and deacons who live there. Though local people give food

and supplies, the monastic community is virtually self-sufficient, growing selected crops and rearing sheep and goats for their milk and meat. The monastery also has its own reservoirs — spectacular caverns hewn deep beneath the surface of the cliff-top centuries ago. It is only possible to explore the full extent of these ancient cisterns during droughts, when they run dry. Usually they are full and coated by a film of green lichen. If you visit them when empty, however, you will find a maze of tunnels and chiselled hollows strikingly reminiscent of the rock-hewn churches of Lalibela.

Above: Breathtaking exterior of the Church of the Redeemer.

Right: Monk studies the scriptures in Lalibela's Church of St Gabriel.

Opposite: Lalibela's rock-hewn Church of the Redeemer.

2. Lalibela: A City Carved from Legend

After the decline of the Axumite empire, lamenting their lost grandeur, Ethiopia's rulers retreated with their Christian subjects to the lofty escarpment of the central uplands. There, protected by mountain battlements more formidable than anything the hand of man could fashion, they were able to repel an increasingly expansionist and militant Islam — trapping and confusing their enemies in the precipitous maze of valleys that intersects the high plateau.

Inevitably, a fortress mentality took root: an intense suspicion of the motives of strangers, a hatred of intrusion and interference, a protective secrecy. During this period — roughly from the seventh to the sixteenth centuries AD — the Ethiopians, encompassed by the enemies of their religion, were described by the British historian Edward Gibbon as having slept for near a thousand years, forgetful of the world by whom they were forgotten. It is true, moreover, that in holding back those who sought to destroy their faith, the highlanders also effectively cut themselves off from the evolving mainstream of Christian culture. This is the only sense, however, in which they slept. Their unique, idiosyncratic civilisation was otherwise very much awake — a singular and spirited affirmation of the creative power of the human intellect.

Many improvisations were so vital, so uplifting, that they have endured to the present day as living expressions of the central and lasting values of Christian Ethiopian culture. Paramount among these priceless legacies, like a great heart beating out an ancient but powerful pulse, is the monastic settlement of Lalibela on a natural 2,600-metre rock terrace surrounded on all sides by rugged and forbidding mountains in the northern extreme of the modern province of Wollo.

Once the thriving and populous capital city of a medieval dynasty, the passing centuries have reduced Lalibela to a village. From the road below, it remains little more than invisible against a horizon dominated by the 4,200-metre peak of Mount Abuna Joseph.

Even close-up it seems wholly unremarkable. It is this camouflaged, chameleon quality, however, that gives the remote settlement its special and lasting place in the life of the highlands — for there, some 800 years ago, safe from the prying eyes and plundering hands of hostile interlopers, a noble king fashioned a secret marvel.

Lalibela, previously known as Roha, is named after the king. The word itself, which translates to mean the bees, recognises his sovereignty and the people of the region still recount the legend that explains why.

Lalibela was born in Roha in the second half of the twelfth century, the youngest son of the royal line of the Zagwe dynasty which then ruled over much of northern Ethiopia. Despite several elder brothers he was destined for greatness from his earliest days. Not long after his birth, his mother found a swarm of bees around his crib and recalled an old belief that the animal world foretold important futures. She cried out: "The bees know that this child will become king."

But trials and tribulations followed. The ruling king feared for his throne and tried to have Lalibela murdered and persecutions continued for several years — culminating in a deadly potion that left the young prince in mortal sleep. During the three-day stupor, Lalibela was transported by angels to the first, second and third heavens where God told him not to worry but to return to Roha and build churches — the like of which the world had never seen before. God also

Above: Preserved ruins of church at Lalibela. Opposite top: (Left) Lalibela monk carries a cross believed to have belonged to King Lalibela. (Right) Monks bear ornate processional crosses among the crowds. Opposite: (Left) Monk with hand cross.(Right) Monk displays priceless illuminated manuscript kept at Debra Damo.

told Lalibela how to design the churches, where to build them and how to decorate them.

Once he was crowned, he gathered masons, carpenters, tools, set down a scale of wages and purchased the land needed for the building. The churches are said to have been built with great speed because angels continued the work at night.

Many scoff at such apocryphal folklore. The Lalibela churches, however, silence the most cynical pedants. These towering edifices were hewn out of the solid, red volcanic tuff on which they stand. In consequence, they seem to be of superhuman creation — in scale, in workmanship and in concept. Close examination is required to appreciate the full extent of the achievement because, like medieval mysteries, much effort has been made to cloak their nature. Some lie almost completely hidden in deep trenches, while others stand in open quarried caves. A complex and bewildering labyrinth of tunnels and narrow passageways with offset crypts, grottoes and galleries connects them all — a cool, lichen-enshrouded, subterranean world, shaded and damp, silent but for the faint echoes of distant footfalls as priests and deacons go about their timeless business.

Four are completely free-standing, attached only to the surrounding rock by their bases. These are Beta Medhane Alem, the House of the Saviour of the World; Beta Ghenetta Mariam, the House of Mary; Beta Ammanuel, the House of Emanuel; and Beta Ghiorghis, the House of St George. Although their individual dimensions and configurations are extremely different, the churches are all built from great blocks of stone, sculptured to resemble normal buildings and wholly isolated within deep courtyards. They represent, as one

authority has put it, "the ultimate in rock-church design . . . . One is amazed at the technical skill, the material resources and the continuity of effort which such vast undertakings imply".

Beta Medhane Alem is particularly striking. More than thirty-three metres long by twenty-three-and-a-half metres wide by eleven metres high it is the largest, surrounded by a colonnade that supports the projecting eaves of the low-pitched, saddle-backed roof. The interior is equally impressive: it has five aisles with flat ceilings, a nave with a barrel vault and eight bays — which are separated by a forest of twenty-eight massive columns. Polished for centuries by the pressure of countless feet, the stone floor reflects shafts of light from apertures in the walls high above.

Nearby Beta Mariam is smaller and less classical than Medhane Alem but inexplicably also more welcoming. A deep square pool in its courtyard is thought to have miraculous properties. At certain seasons — notably Christmas — women who cannot conceive dip themselves in its algae-covered waters. Dedicated to Mary, the mother of Christ, this church is fifteen metres long by eleven metres wide by ten metres high. Alone among the Lalibela monoliths, it has a projecting porch. Internally, it is dominated by a tall pier in the centre of the transept which supports the barrel vault of the nave. The remains of early unusual frescoes are on the ceiling and upper walls and there are many elaborately carved details on the piers, capitals and arches.

Further away, Beta Ammanuel is approached through a tunnel within a deep and narrow courtyard. The exterior of the church, much praised by art-historians, is extremely elaborate. The walls are carved in courses, alternately recessed and projecting — mimicking the timber and plastered-stone layers

Above: Treasured frescoes in one of Lalibela's rock-hewn churches.

Opposite: Midday sun falls on a monk rapt in study.

of traditional Ethiopian architecture. Internally there are five bays — and a double row of piers separate the nave from the aisles. The nave's upper walls have a handsome frieze and, above this, windows which open into the sanctuary and the lofts over the aisles.

Beta Ghiorghis, the last of the truly monolithic churches of Lalibela, rests a considerable distance from all the others in majestic isolation. Standing more than twelve metres high in the centre of a deep, almost well-like pit, externally and internally it resembles a Greek cross. There is a faultless dome over the sanctuary, decorated with a *croix patte* in relief, and the craftsmanship throughout is superb. Legend has it that St George — on horseback and in full armour — supervised the excavation of this remarkable church. The hoofmarks of his horse are still proudly pointed out in the courtyard by the resident monks.

As well as the four monolithic churches, Lalibela has seven other rock-hewn edifices which demonstrate various degrees of separation from the surrounding volcanic tuff. Beta Abba Libanos, for example, is semi-detached — all its four walls are isolated but the roof merges into the cliff above. By contrast, Beta Golgotha, the House of Golgotha, and Beta Qedus Mikael, the House of St Michael, are much more subterranean — although the latter has three exposed facades and the former has one. The remaining churches are Beta Dengel, House of the Virgins; Beta Selassie, House of the Trinity; Beta Qedus Mercurios, House of St Mercurios; and Beta Qedus Gabriel-Rufael, House of St Gabriel and St Raphael. In addition, several other arresting rock-hewn features are not churches — among them the so-called Tomb of Adam, a huge rectangular block of stone, hollowed out internally, which

stands in a deep trench in front of the western face of Beta Golgotha.

All in all, the Lalibela monoliths represent the finest flowering of an old art-form — other examples of which may be found throughout highland Ethiopia. The architects were skilled and knowledgeable at a level that does not exist today. But it is highly improbable their labours were completed, as the legend insists, in just twenty-four years. The work probably continued long after Lalibela's death. Indeed, in his memory, Queen Maskal Kabra, his wife, is said to have built Beta Abba Libanos — with the help of angels, of course — in just one night. Certain features also suggest later additions. Historical detail, hard facts and precise dates are all elusive in so mythical and enigmatic a place. Nonetheless, as the scholar David Buxton observed, all who visit there will continue to marvel at the mind that conceived so grandiose a plan, and at the endless patient labour that carried it through to completion.

The first European to visit Lalibela was Francisco Alvarez, a Portuguese friar, who arrived in the 1520s on an expedition to convert the Coptic Abyssinians to the Roman Church. Overwhelmed by this remote mountain stronghold — perhaps because it so completely contradicted his notions of European cultural superiority — he was convinced his peers would disbelieve his account. He concluded his report: "I swear by God, in whose power I am, that all that is written is the truth, and there is much more than I have already written, and I have left it that they may not tax me with its being falsehood."

In fact, each of Lalibela's churches is an architectural prodigy. Beyond that, it is a place where the whole adds up to a far greater sum than its parts — remarkable though those

Above: Aerial view of Lalibela.

Left: St George's Church at Lalibela seen from on high.

Opposite: Steps lead to the carved rock refuge of a Lalibela monk.

parts are. In a sense, the entire magnificient conception is one single piece of living sculpture — a prayer of stone, an immense, composite work carved with serene inspiration, dedicated to eternal glory.

Surviving remnants of an ineffable past, the Lalibela churches testify to the power and spirit of an archaic Christian faith — one that retains its hold on hearts and minds in the Ethiopian north, at the end of the second millennium, with a pristine and undiminished vigour. There, throughout the year, worshippers bare their souls to the Almighty and celebrate and reaffirm the shared values of their widely scattered highland communities.

The most heavily attended services are in the early morning, around dawn, before the arduous work in the fields begins. In the chill grey light, one leaves the modern age behind, slipping back into primordial solemnity. The rhythmical music has a ponderous undertone of drums and tambourines coupled to the chant of the deacons and the congregation calling out for God's mercy, while the cold, dark walls, rough stone floor and the silhouettes leaning on prayer sticks or slumped in obeisance seem to constitute a direct, unbroken link with elsewhere and elsewhen. It is easy to understand the commanding call of early Christianity and how it fired the imagination of millions. The church performed miracles, healed the sick and raised the dead. In this context, the feeding of the 5,000, the story of Lazarus, and of Christ walking on the water, all appear perfectly comprehensible. Indeed, many who come to Lalibela's rock-hewn churches still unquestioningly believe that miracles stem from the pure energy of faith focussed through the lives of saints and holy men.

Lalibela's role as a place of active worship becomes

particularly clear at Christmas which, according to Ethiopia's Julian Calendar, takes place in early January, and at Epiphany, which is celebrated twelve days later. Even in the hardest times, tens of thousands of pilgrims walk for days, even months, from far-off hamlets in inaccessible valleys, at their own pace, with their own preoccupations, to be there.

The unadulterated biblical atmosphere, and vivid local colour of the *Timkat* (Epiphany) celebrations provide an ideal opportunity to see Lalibela as a sacred centre whose roots go back to antiquity. Indeed, while *Timkat* commemorates John's baptism of Christ in the waters of the River Jordan, the central symbolism of the great annual ritual revolves around processions in which the sacred *tabots* — representations of the Ark of the Covenant and wrapped in rich brocades — are brought out for the people to see.

72

Above: Timkat celebrants crowd the walls and entrance of St Georges Church, Lalibela.

Opposite top: Brightly coloured parasols symbolise the joy of Timkat at Lalibela.
Opposite: Exterior of Lalibela church.

73

3. Gondar

The next stop on the Historic Route is the graceful city of Gondar, founded by Emperor Fasilidas around 1635. It is famous for its many medieval castles and the design and decoration of its churches — in particular, Debra Berhan Selassie which represents a masterpiece of the Gondarene school of art.

Famous though Gondar may be, however, no one knows exactly why Fasilidas chose to establish his headquarters there. Some legends say an archangel prophesied that an Ethiopian capital would be built at a place with a name that began with the letter G. The legend led to a whole series of sixteenth- and seventeenth-century towns — Guzara, Gorgora and finally Gondar. Another legend claims that the city was built in a place chosen by God. Apparently, He pointed it out to Fasilidas who was on a hunting expedition and followed a buffalo to the spot.

Flanked by twin mountain streams at an altitude of more than 2,300 metres, Gondar commands spectacular views over farmlands to the gleaming waters of Lake Tana thirty-five kilometres to the south. The city retains an atmosphere of antique charm mingled with an aura of mystery and violence. An extensive compound, near its centre, contains the hulking ruins of a group of imposing castles like some African Camelot. The battlements and towers evoke images of chivalrous knights on horseback and of ceremonies laden with pageantry and honour. Other, darker, reverberations recall chilling echoes of Machiavellian plots and intrigues, tortures and poisonings.

The main castle was built in the late 1630s and early 1640s on the orders of Fasilidas. The Emperor, who was greatly interested in architecture — St Mary's in Axum was another of

his works — was also responsible for seven churches, a number of bridges, and a three-storey stone pavilion next to a large, sunken bathing place, rectangular in shape, which is still filled during the *Timkat* season with water from the nearby Qaha river.

Other structures date from later periods. Iyasu the Great, a grandson of Fasilidas, was particularly active. His castle, centrally located in the main compound, was described at the time by his chronicler as finer than the House of Solomon. Its inner walls were decorated with ivory, mirrors and paintings of palm trees, its ceiling covered with gold-leaf and precious stones. Now gutted, haunted only by ghosts, the intact turrets and towers of this fine stronghold reflect its past glory.

Iyasu's most lasting achievement, was the Church of Debra Berhan Selassie, the Light of the Trinity, which stands, surrounded by a high wall, on raised ground to the north-west of the city and continues to be in regular use. A plain, thatched, rectangular structure on the outside, the interior of Debra Berhan Selassie is marvellously painted with a great many scenes from religious history. The spaces between the beams of the ceiling contain the brilliant wide-eyed images of more than eighty angels' faces — all different, with their own character and expressions. The north wall, in which is the holy of holies, is dominated by a depiction of the Trinity above the crucifixion. The theme of the south wall is St Mary; that of the east wall the life of Jesus. The west wall shows important saints, with St George in red-and-gold on a prancing white horse.

Not long after completing this remarkable and impressive work, Iyasu went into deep depression when his favourite concubine died. He abandoned affairs of state and his son,

Above: Timkat ceremony at Gondar.

Opposite: Timkat festival at Gondar, beside a palace sometimes attributed to Emperor Fasilidas.

Tekla Haimanot, responded by declaring himself Emperor. Shortly afterwards, in 1706, his father was assassinated on his orders.

In turn, Tekla Haimanot was murdered. His successor was also forcibly deposed and the next monarch was poisoned. The brutalities came to an end with Emperor Bakaffa who left two fine castles — one attributed directly to him and one to his consort, the Empress Mentewab.

Bakaffa's successor, Iyasu II, is regarded by most historians as the last of the Gondar Emperors to rule with full authority. During his reign, work began on a whole range of new buildings outside the main palace compound. The monarch also developed the hills north-west of the city centre known as Kweskwam — after the home of the Virgin Mary. Most buildings there are in ruins today, including the largest — a square, three-storey castle with a flat roof and crenellated walls embellished with a series of bas-reliefs of various Ethiopian animals.

After Iyasu II in the mid-1700s, the realm sank into increasing chaos with regular *coups d'etat* and the rise of a rebellious nobility who became dominant in Ethiopian national life.

The story of Gondar, however, amounts to a great deal more than the annals of the monarchs who ruled there or chronicles of their rivalries and intrigues.

While it remained the capital of Ethiopia until 1855, the city was a vigorous and vital centre of religious learning and art. Painting and music, dance and poetry, together with skilled instruction in these and many other disciplines, thrived for more than two hundred years. At the end of the eighteenth century a poet declaimed:

Beautiful from its beginnings, Gondar, hope of the wretched!
And hope of the Great, Gondar without measure or bounds!
O dove of John, Gondar, generous-hearted, mother!
Gondar, never bowed by affliction!
Gondar with its merry name!
Gondar, seat of prosperity and of savoury food!
Gondar, dwelling of King Iyasu and of mighty Bakaffa!
Gondar, which emulated the City of David, the land of Salem!
She will be a myth unto eternity!

Gondar's rise to prominence under Fasilidas occurred little less than a century after Ethiopian Christendom had come close to total destruction at the hands of the Islamic warlord, Ahmed Gragn, whose forces swept in from the east in 1528. The fighting only ended in 1543 when the Muslim commander was shot dead by a Portuguese musketeer — one of 400 who had been sent to reinforce the flagging armies of Emperor Galawdewos.

Narrating Gragn's fate, the British traveller Sir Richard Burton wrote: "Thus perished the African hero who dashed to pieces the structure of 2,500 years." It was no exaggeration. Gragn's *Jihad* was a national catastrophe for Ethiopia. The Christian highlands, from Axum in the north to the shores of Lake Tana in the west, were almost completely overrun for more than a decade and much of the cultural legacy of previous centuries disappeared. In a sustained orgy of vandalism, hundreds of churches — great artistic treasure-houses — were looted and burnt and an immense booty carried away.

Gondar, beautiful from its beginnings, rose from the ashes of this smouldering backdrop of so recent and so traumatic a

Above: Entrance to Church of Debra Berhan Selassie at Gondar.
Opposite top: Sunshine dapples exterior of Church of Debra Berhan Selassie, at Gondar.
Opposite: Richly decorated ceiling of Church of Debra Berhan Selassie, with picture of three old men representing the Trinity.

81

history. There can be little doubt that Fasilidas and his successors saw their elegant capital as a phoenix and so patronised the arts. They were doing nothing less than rebuilding their national heritage. In the process they built faithfully on the few solid foundations left from the past, rediscovered much that had been thought lost, and established a sense of purpose and a new direction for the future.

Sculpture, as one authority observes, makes little appeal to the Ethiopians, who have, however, a pronounced interest in pictorial art. This fascination with painting, mainly expressed through church murals, icons, illuminated manuscripts and scrolls, has been long sustained. It dates back to the beginnings of the Christian era at least; but the depradations of Gragn and other invaders mean that relatively little from earlier than the sixteenth century has been preserved.

From what is available, academics have identified two principal epochs. The first is known as the medieval, with paintings that have origins in a remote past. The surviving exemplars date roughly from the thirteenth to the early sixteenth centuries, before Gragn. The second period, referred to as Gondarene, began in the seventeenth century with the founding of the city. Despite the subsequent introduction of a number of important innovations, this period extends through to modern times.

The medieval school of Ethiopian painting was dominated by Byzantine influences. By contrast, the identifying hallmark of the Gondarene period is an increasingly Western European approach. The difference between the two styles and, indeed, between contemporary Ethiopian art and works executed in antiquity, is not so very great. One leading expert says it is surprising how invariable are the basic canons of the

traditional Ethiopian painter. They have not changed substantially in the last six centuries, which gives us good reason to believe that they were the same a thousand years ago.

Confronted with a collection of Ethiopian paintings dating from several widely separated centuries, the layman is most likely to be struck by the essential similarities that link all the works. Furthermore, the unifying impetus that shines through all the paintings is essentially Ethiopian: an indigenous input of great force and originality.

Religious themes dominate all but the most recent Ethiopian art, hardly surprising since painting was introduced into the country along with Christianity. In particular, the Holy Scriptures were imported exclusively from the Byzantine world and were illuminated, naturally, in the Byzantine style. Thereafter, from generation to generation, they were translated and recopied in Ethiopian churches and monasteries.

It was inevitable, given that calligraphers and decorators were essentially copyists, that the works of the medieval period should so strongly reflect Byzantine rules. Thus, for example, the rigid and lifeless persons depicted are indicators of spiritual hierarchy. The centre-ground of almost every painting is occupied by the principal character in the scriptural story told. Invariably, colours used fall within a limited range — green, red, yellow and blue — and, again, this is in accord with the criteria of the Byzantine world.

Despite such restrictions, Ethiopian artists of the medieval school managed to interpret their genre in a fresh and individual manner. What they sought was not to represent or mimic reality but to manifest their religious belief and feelings

Above: Young novice monk displays pages of one of Gondar's priceless illuminated manuscripts.

Right: Coffin of the eighteenth-century Empress of Mentewab in one of Gondar's churches.

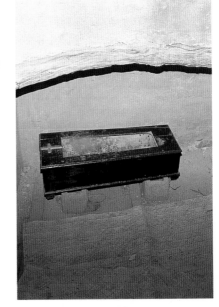

Opposite: Ruins of the palace of Empress Mentewab at Kweskwam overlooking Gondar.

through colour and design. One particularly effective convention among their original contributions was the presentation of good in full face and of evil in profile.

Even after the demise of the medieval period and the foundation of Gondar, scriptural themes maintained their importance in Ethiopian art. The range of stories, however, increased dramatically. The Virgin Mary became an increasingly popular subject as did the lives and acts of the saints. Stylistically, from the beginning there was a willingness to adopt new models — for example Renaissance or Baroque paintings. These models emanated from the expansive and powerful Western civilisations with which Ethiopia came into contact from the sixteenth century. Naturalism became more acceptable and a conscious effort was made by at least some artists to depart from stiff and geometrical Byzantine lines. Perspective and relief were introduced, together with motion and elaborate details. This new realism also brought with it an eagerness to depict the Ethiopian way of life, thus surrounding even the most spiritual subjects you may sometimes distinguish the presence of everyday objects such as houses, weapons and baskets. Most notable of all is the manner in which the personalities depicted in the best Gondarene works are no longer flat or inanimate but full of life. Eyes that were immobile move in different directions, bodies bend and hands express feeling.

These lifelike qualities — combined with a Baroque richness of design, a warmth of colour and a careful finish — distinguish the dazzling paintings of the Debra Berhan Selassie church in Gondar. The same may also be said of another fine group of paintings in the church of Debra Sina at Gorgora — an ancient settlement on the northern shores of

Lake Tana. Although this large, thatched edifice was built during the early years of the fourteenth century, its interior was extensively restored by Emperor Fasilidas, his sister Woizero Meleko Tawit and various successors. As a result the Debra Sina murals belong firmly to the Gondarene rather than the medieval period.

Above: Massive ramparts and walls of the Fasilidas castle at Gondar.
Opposite top: Battlements and turrets of Gondar's castles and churches dominate the mountain skyline around the city.
Opposite: Ethiopia's highlands stretch out beyond Gondar.

4. Lake Tana, the Blue Nile Falls and Bahar Dar

Restorative work also explains the Gondarene character of some of the paintings found in the remarkable monasteries and churches on the islands of Lake Tana. Kebran Gabriel, for example, originally established in the fourteenth century, was later renovated and rebuilt during the reign of Emperor Iyasu I (1682-1706). Narga Selassie, built in the eighteenth century by Empress Mentewab, is also Gondarene in character. Other churches are influenced by different periods. For instance, although Ura Kidane Mehret on the Zegie Peninsula is a fourteenth-century building, its most powerful murals — notably around the holy of holies — were painted in Gondarene times. On the other hand, the centrepiece of Daga Istafanos is a Madonna painted during the reign of Emperor Zara Yaqob (1434-68). Although medieval by date, this work has the flowing lines, realism, beauty and tension of much later styles.

The thirty-seven islands of Lake Tana shelter twenty monasteries — surviving remnants of an old, contemplative tradition. Because of their isolation they were used to store art treasures and religious relics from all parts of the country. Tradition says the Ark of the Covenant was kept on one of these islands when Axum was endangered, and the remains of five Emperors — including Fasilidas — are to be found at Daga Istafanos. Monks at Ura Kidane Mehret say that more than forty *tabots* from churches destroyed by Ahmed Gragn were hidden in their monastery during the sixteenth century.

Covering more than 3,600 square kilometres, Tana is Ethiopia's largest lake. Known to the ancient Greeks as Pseboa, its sometimes stormy waters are traversed by papyrus reed boats, called *tankwas*, which differ little from those depicted on the tombs of the Pharaohs. Appropriately enough,

the Blue Nile river flows out of the lake with tremendous force and volume over the basalt shoulder of a giant cataract and onwards from there, ever downwards through dark and angry defiles, towards the deserts of the Sudan, on its way to enrich Egypt's fertile delta.

The power of the Blue Nile may best be appreciated just thirty kilometres downstream from the point where the river first leaves Lake Tana. There, a rumble of sound fills the air and the green fields and low hills on either bank tremble to the Blue Nile Falls. It is one of the most dramatic spectacles on either the White or Blue Niles, a vision of natural strength and grandeur.

Four hundred metres wide in flood, the Blue Nile plunges forty-five metres down a sheer chasm to throw up a continuous mist that drenches the countryside up to a kilometre away. In turn, this gentle deluge produces rainbows that shimmer across the gorge under the changing arc of the sun — and a perennial rainforest. The pillar of cloud in the sky above, seen from afar, explains the local name for the falls — water that smokes, *Tissisat*.

The approach to the falls leads through Tissisat village where travellers find themselves surrounded by a retinue of youthful guides. For a small fee, they will point out many places of historic interest.

From the village the footpath meanders beside open and fertile fields before it drops into a deep basaltic rift spanned by an ancient, fortified seventeenth-century stone bridge built by Portuguese adventurers.

A stiff climb up a grassy hillside under the blue and breathless sky follows. Finally, the falls come into view, the smooth, majestic edge of the rolling Nile breaking into a

Above: Religious ritual at one of the island monasteries of Lake Tana.

Opposite: Sundown over Lake Tana.

thundering cataract of white water foaming and boiling down a dark cliff.

Different people at different times have written with awe and wonder of the spectacle that the Blue Nile Falls presents. Most, mesmerised by the sight, leave in a mood of respectful contemplation. "The river", wrote the Scottish traveller James Bruce in 1770, "fell in one sheet of water, without any interval, above half an English mile in breadth, with a force and a noise that was truly terrible and which stunned and made me, for a time, perfectly dizzy. A thick fume, or haze, covered the Fall all round and hung over the course of the stream both above and below, marking its track, though the water was not seen. It was a magnificent sight that ages, added to the greatest length of human life, would not efface or eradicate from my memory; it struck me with a kind of stupor, and a total oblivion of where I was, and of every other sublunary concern."

For the modern traveller, the starting point of any visit to the Blue Nile Falls, or to the islands of Lake Tana, is the bustling market town of Bahar Dar on the lake's south-eastern shore. Although pretty enough, with wide, palm-lined avenues and gardens overflowing with tropical vegetation, the town has little historic interest. But its colourful markets, and a variety of handicrafts and weaving centres, make it a comfortable base for excursions — either by land or by water.

The visitor to Bahar Dar may be interested to see Ethiopia's first two-storey building. It is situated within the precincts of the modern Ethiopian Orthodox church of St George beside the lake. This fine old structure was built in the early seventeenth century by a Spanish Jesuit, Pero Paes, who came, unsuccessfully to convert the country to Catholicism.

The overland route to the falls is about forty-five minutes by vehicle to Tissisat village and another forty-five minutes on foot. Those who wish to visit the monastic islands, however, have no alternative but to hire one of the boats owned by the Maritime Authority located at Bahar Dar Port, opposite the Ethiopian Airlines office.

The *MV Dahlak* carries visitors to the nearest monastery, Kebran Gabriel, in less than an hour. The island juts out from the water like the tip of a submerged mountain planted over with rich green trees. There is only one landfall — a jetty from which a well-trodden path winds upwards under a canopy of branches. No women are allowed to set foot there, but male travellers may visit the island without formality.

The monastery is at the top of the island in a stone-walled compound dominated by a large, circular church in traditional Ethiopic design, with walls of compacted mud and straw. This unassuming building, nevertheless, has a cathedral atmosphere as impressive as that evoked by the great European places of worship like Notre Dame or Westminster Abbey.

Kebran Gabriel is renowned for a magnificent manuscript of the Four Gospels which, according to the art historian Stanislaw Chojnacki, sometime Curator of the Institute of Ethiopian Studies Museum, is believed to date back to at least the late fourteenth or early fifteenth century. This is one of the Ethiopian Church's many historic treasures, a large number of which are housed on the islands of Lake Tana. Ethiopian churchmen over the centuries have faithfully guarded such works with remarkable dedication and, in not a few cases, literally gave their lives in their protection.

Another monastery within an hour's cruise of Bahar Dar is

Above: Monk guards the entrance to a Lake Tana island monastery.
Opposite top: Colourful fresco adorns walls of Ura Kidane Mehret Monastery, Lake Tana.
Opposite: Stunning frescoes found in Ura Kidane Mehret Monastery, Lake Tana.

Ura Kidane Mehret, situated on the Zegie Peninsula. Because it is part of the mainland its outlook is different from that of Kebran Gabriel. There is less emphasis on isolation and the monastery is clearly part of the local community, with children playing in its green and leafy compound and villagers who come and go freely. Women are allowed and the monks are open and communicative.

The church's design is similar to Kebran Gabriel and, indeed, dates from the same period. But it is more decorative with a huge, conical thatched roof and it is painted inside and out with colourful frescoes depicting scenes from biblical lore and from the history of the Ethiopian Orthodox Church.

The visitor should look out for the peninsula's many coffee bushes, from which beans were in the old days transported to Gondar for export to the Sudan or to the Red Sea port of Massawa.

The third principal tourist attraction among the islands of Lake Tana is Daga Istafanos which, like Kebran Gabriel, is closed to women. Perhaps ninety minutes cruise from Bahar Dar, its steep sides are densely forested with gnarled, ancient trees. A winding path leads upwards to the monastery on the summit. You may notice, as you climb, that the air is laden with the loamy scent of freshly turned earth and the fragrance of tropical flowers. The hum of bees and other large insects fills the air and, in the distance, you may hear the monotonous ringing of a traditional stone bell announcing the time of prayer.

Eventually, some ninety metres above the surface of the lake, you come across some low round buildings with thatched roofs. This is where the monks live. Next you pass under an arch set into a high stone wall and finally enter a grassy clearing at the centre of which stands the church of Saint Stephanos. It is a long rectangular structure, curved at the ends, with a covered walkway extending all around it. It was built about a century ago after the original was destroyed by a grass fire.

Its historic interest lies in the contents of its treasury — a largish, stone structure next to the church with a massive wooden door closed by a hulking, antique lock opened with a huge iron key.

It is quite dark inside and you need candles or flashlights to see your way. When you have grown accustomed to the gloom, however, you will find that you can make out many piles of brightly coloured ceremonial robes and several rows of shelves bearing substantial boxes ranged around the walls. These are the coffins and mummified remains of several former Emperors of Ethiopia. In the order of their reigns, they are Yekuno Amlak, who restored the Solomonic dynasty to the throne in 1270; Dawit, late fourteenth century; Zara Yaqob, fifteenth century; Za Dengel, early seventeenth century; and Fasilidas, also seventeenth century.

All the coffins are equipped with glass sides. Donated by Haile Selassie in the 1950s they replaced the originals which were rotting away. The glass provides a fish-tank view of the mummified bodies. Four are now skeletons, with only a few scraps of parchment-like flesh. The fifth still has recognisable features. It is Fasilidas, the founder of Gondar.

Considered one of the most sacred islands on Lake Tana, Daga Istafanos is said to have served as a temporary hiding place for the Ark of the Covenant in the sixteenth century when the forces of the Muslim warlord Ahmed Gragn attacked and occupied Axum. Another island on the lake has

an even stronger claim to the Ark. Tana Kirkos lies off the reed-fringed eastern shore about two-and-a-half hours cruise north of Bahar Dar.

A beautiful and unusual place, Tana Kirkos is completely covered by dense green shrubbery, flowering trees and tall cactus plants. It rises steeply from the water to a high peak on which there is a thatched, circular house. Sunbirds, kingfishers and bright blue starlings dart through the air. On the shore of a small sandy bay, smiling monks, alerted by the sound of the boat's engine, stand on a makeshift jetty to meet visitors. They escort them up a narrow, overgrown path, cut out of the side of a grey cliff, past an ancient and somewhat dilapidated church dedicated to Saint Cherkos — after whom the monastery is named — through an archway, and into a clearing containing three or four houses where the island's entire population — about a dozen monks and deacons — have their homes.

There you will be shown the treasures of the island which consist of many beautiful illuminated scrolls and leather-bound books with leather pages hand-lettered in *Ge'ez*. By far the greatest treasure, however, is a powerful oral tradition which the monks inherited from their predecessors, handed down through many ages. This tells how the Ark of the Covenant was first brought here for safekeeping. The monks claim that the Ark rested on their island for eight hundred years as the centrepiece of an influential and extensive Jewish cult until Ethiopia was converted to Christianity. Only then was the sacred relic removed to its present resting place at Axum and its symbolism incorporated into the rituals and ceremonies of the Ethiopian Orthodox Church. Since the date of Ethiopia's conversion to Christianity was around AD 350 the

implication is that the Ark must have arrived on Tana Kirkos eight hundred years before then.

The monks may well show you the place where the Ark rested and the sacrificial altars placed before it. These stand high on the cliff overlooking Lake Tana near the summit of the island, on a raised plinth made of natural unhewn rock. There three short stone pillars are grouped closely together. The tallest — perhaps a metre-and-a-half high — is square with a cup hollowed out of the top. The other two, each about a metre high, are circular in section and as thick as a man's thigh. They have also been hollowed out at the top to a depth of about ten centimetres. The monks claim that rams were sacrificed in the presence of the Ark and the blood poured over the pillars.

The traveller with time, could spend weeks exploring for the the treasures of Lake Tana and its many islands.

Above: Rare illuminated religious scripture in a Lake Tana island monastery.

Left: Many monks spend their lives in the solitude of the monasteries on the remote islands of Lake Tana.

Above: Ethiopia has a rich legacy of religious art, found in churches and monasteries throughout the country.

5. Harar

No journey along Ethiopia's fabled historic route would be complete without a visit to the medieval walled city of Harar which stands amid green mountains on the east wall of the Great Rift Valley near the Somali border. Unlike the great cultural centres of the Christian highlands, Harar's heritage is almost entirely Muslim and Oriental. For centuries it has served as a bridgehead for the entry of Islamic ideas into Africa from the nearby Arabian peninsula. Almost equally important for the character of this unique city is the fact that it has always enjoyed close connections with the Somali coast and with trade from the Indian subcontinent.

To understand Harar's special flavour it is necessary to step back in time for some idea of the trade that gave this colourful emporium its heyday. In the nineteenth century, much of that trade came overland from Berbera in the Gulf of Aden. One eyewitness account of the 1840s describes the fat and wealthy Banian traders from Porebunder, Mandavie and Bombay, who rolled across [the Indian Ocean] in their clumsy *Kotias* in order to attend the Berbera fair. With a formidable row of empty ghee jars slung over the quarters of their vessels, these aggressive merchants apparently elbowed themselves into a permanent position in the front tier of craft in the harbour and, by their superior capital, cunning and influence, soon distanced all competitors.

Another observer at the fair, CW Harris, wrote of the rapacious Banians and declared that these subtle traders had enjoyed silently, and unobserved, the enormous profits accruing from the riches annually poured out from the hidden regions of Africa. Writing with a pen that was tainted with the prejudices of his age, Harris tells us that the curious stalls of the fat Banians from India were thronged from morning until night with barbarians from adjacent districts, who brought animal skins and drugs to be exchanged; "and the clamour of haggling and barter was hourly increased by the arrival of some new caravan of toil-worn pedlars from the remote depths of the interior, each laden with an accession of rich merchandise to be converted into baubles and blue calico, at a clear net profit to the specious Hindoo of 200 per cent. Myrrh, ivory, and gum Arabic; civet, frankincense and ostrich feathers were piled in every corner of his booth; and the tearing of ells of Nils stuff and Surat cloth, and the counting of porcelain beads, was incessant so long as the daylight lasted."

However outrageous the cheating that went on at the fair, and however inflated the prices, the bulk of the merchandise eventually found its way inland to yield even greater profits to even more unscrupulous merchants. Travellers' tales from the 1850s suggest that during the trading season caravans of up to 5,000 heavily burdened camels left Berbera every day and journeyed west to Harar. There the merchandise would be put on sale in exotic market places or else repacked for distribution throughout Africa. With clear resentment for the great profits being raked in by the traders of Harar, Somali nomads of the time characterised the beautiful walled city as a paradise inhabited by asses.

Despite its somewhat isolated position, Harar has probably always had a great deal more in common with the Horn's cosmopolitan coastal culture than with the life of the highlands — and it retains to this day a certain redolence of the Orient. In 1854, the British adventurer Sir Richard Burton became the first European to be allowed to enter the town. He disliked the Emir at first sight and later described him as resembling a little Indian Rajah, an etiolated youth twenty-four or twenty-five

years old, plain and thin bearded, with a yellowed complexion, wrinkled brows and protruding eyes. The ruler's only redeeming feature was his dress — a flowing robe of crimson cloth, edged with snowy fur, and a narrow white turban tightly twisted round a tall conical cap of red velvet, like the old Turkish headgear of our painters.

Burton's antipathy also extended to almost all other Harari males, whether noble or lowly-born. "Their features", he commented, "are coarse and debauched; many of them squint, others have lost an eye by small-pox, and they are disfigured by scrofula and other diseases. The women, however, appeared better favoured: They have regular profiles, straight noses, large eyes, mouths approaching the Caucasian type, and light yellow complexions. Dress here is a disguise to charms . . . . Women of the upper class, when leaving the house, throw a blue sheet over the head, which, however, is rarely veiled. The front and back hair, parted in the centre, is gathered into two large bunches below the ears, and covered with dark blue muslin or network, whose ends meet under the chin . . . . The virgins collect their locks, which are generally wavy not wiry, and grow long as well as thick, into a knot tied *à la Diane* behind the head . . . . The ear is decorated with Somali rings or red coral beads, the neck with necklaces of the same material, and the forearms with six or seven of the broad circles of buffalo and other dark horns prepared in Western India. Finally stars are tatooed upon the bosom, the eyebrows are lengthened with dies, the eyes fringed with kohl, and the hands and feet stained with henna."

After Burton's visit to what he called the East African counterpart of ill-famed Timbucktoo, many other Europeans followed his pioneering footsteps from the coast to Harar. In the late nineteenth century, for example, Arthur Rimbaud lived in the city, writing erotic verses for his public, sending complaining letters to his mother, and still finding time to trade in silks, cottons, coffee, gum, perfumes, ivory and gold. The strange Gothic residence that the eccentric French poet is (wrongly) said to have occupied still stands — its stained-glass windows overlook the old Megalo Gudo bazaar where shrewd Harari market women play the role of latter-day Banians offering for sale fine headcloths of Indian muslin and conducting a profitable business in locally-made silver, gold and amber jewellery, as well as in beads, baubles and cheap metal trinkets imported from Bombay and Delhi.

With its ninety mosques and shrines, Harar is considered to be the fourth most sacred centre of the Islamic world. It was established in the early sixteenth century by a local chief, Sultan Abu Bakr Muhammad, and was shortly afterwards besieged and captured by the fanatical Muslim leader Ahmed Gragn. From there he went on to launch his devastating holy war against the Christian Ethiopian highlands. In 1543, however, in a decisive battle on the shores of Lake Tana, Gragn was shot dead by a certain Peter de Leon — a musketeer of low stature but passing valiant — who belonged to the expeditionary force that had been sent by the King of Portugal to assist the Ethiopian Emperor.

After his sudden demise, the forces of the Muslim warlord scattered and political power in Harar was assumed by his widow, Bati Del Wambara, who married her late husband's nephew, Nur ibn al-Wazir Mujahid. Together they attempted to continue the *Jihad* against the Christians but the tables had now decisively turned and subsequent years saw Harar surrounded and, on one occasion penetrated, by Christian

Previous page: The great mosque in Harar.
Overleaf: The medieval walled city of Harar
stands amid green mountains on the east wall
of the Great Rift Valley.

forces. It was at this time that the formidable defensive walls which still encircle the city were built. Their five massive gateways also still stand.

Despite being weakened by the war with the Christians, Harar continued to be an important emirate and still had about it an aura of mystery, power and charm. When Sir Richard Burton succeeded in visiting it in 1854, he was particularly impressed by its walls and gates which, he confirmed, were "at all times . . . . carefully guarded." In the evenings, apparently, the gates were securely locked and the keys taken to the Emir — after which no one could enter or leave the city until dawn.

Then, as now, the chief building within the walls was the great mosque, known as Al-Jami. Burton, familiar with finer structures elsewhere in the Middle East, described it somewhat patronisingly and unfairly as a large barn of poverty-stricken appearance . . . with two whitewashed minarets of truncated conoid shape. The latter may still be seen across the surrounding countryside from some distance by any traveller approaching from the east.

Some years after Burton's visit, Harar's independent statehood was brought to an end by Emperor Menelik II of Ethiopia who incorporated the walled city into his rapidly-expanding empire. Menelik made his intentions known in June 1885 when he announced to the world: "We have no intention of looting or destroying. After taking Harar, we will protect and govern everyone according to his religion. We will subdue and pacify the route from Shoa to the sea. That is what we intend to do."

Not until the end of the following year, however, did Menelik finally muster his forces and march on Harar. He

114

tried at first to persuade the city's ruler, Emir Abd Allahi, to surrender without a fight as other local rulers had done and soon would do. But the chief was obdurate. The decisive battle, which resulted in the Emir's absolute defeat, took place on 6 January 1887. Soon afterwards Menelik entered the city and appointed his own cousin — Ras Makonnen, the father of Haile Selassie — as Governor. Determined to avoid sectarian strife, Menelik nevertheless entrusted most aspects of the local administration to the former Emir's nephew Ali, who had previously been imprisoned by his uncle, and issued a decree stating that the citizens, whatever their faith, should live in accordance with their religious traditions and beliefs.

Harar continued to flourish as a trading emporium throughout the early years of the twentieth century. It declined with the building of the Addis Ababa-Djibouti railway which bypassed the ancient walled city. Commerce tended, as a result, to be increasingly diverted to the nearby railway town of Dire Dawa. It was even known for a time as New Harar, *Addis Harar*.

Nevertheless, Harar has managed to retain its medieval character and charm and its past glory amid the ebb and flow of conquering armies and is now a fascinating stopover for the traveller. It has an ethnically complex population made up of Adaris, the indigenous highland Ethiopian people of this region who speak a Semitic language related to Amharic, Arabs, Oromos and Somalis from the plains. This cultural diversity is best expressed in the old market at the centre of the city where tall, graceful maidens in long, flowing, extravagantly coloured dresses come to barter and buy amongst the elegant Moorish archways.

Rightly renowned for its intricately worked filigree jewellery

of silver, gold and amber, Harar's Megalo Gudo market is also a centre for beautiful baskets of woven grass, decorative wall-mats and bright shawls, as well as fruit, vegetables, spices and grains of the province. Outwards, a warren of steep, narrow, cobbled alleyways twists from the market between ancient balconied houses where travellers may wander until they reach one of the five gates in the city wall.

Harar's Islamic character is best expressed in the Grand Mosque (Al-Jami), which dominates the town. Though neither large nor elaborate by Middle Eastern standards, Burton's nineteenth-century description of it as a poverty-stricken barn was unkind and inaccurate. Built on sixteenth-century foundations, its tall, whitewashed minarets soar skywards above a broad courtyard in which pilgrims cleanse themselves. The cool and spacious interior, dimly illuminated by shafts of sunlight entering through the open windows, is filled with the whisper of prayer and the click of rosary beads as worshippers recount the ninety-nine names of God.

Near the mosque, as though in fulfilment of Menelik II's vow to honour religious tolerance in the city, stands the imposing octagonal cathedral of Medhane Alem which the emperor built when he captured the city in 1887. The cathedral contains a gallery of traditional religious art.

Also worth visiting are the palace of Ras Makonnen, Harar's first governor, the tomb of Abu Said, an early Muslim leader, and the colourful Shoa Gate market.

Above: Gateway into the walled city of Harar. Overleaf: Old castles of Gondar. Following pages: Colourful celebrants at the Timkat Festival. Pages 124-5: The old bridge of Emporor Fasilidas on the way to Tissisat, or Blue Nile, Falls. Pages 126-7: Sundown over the Blue Nile. Page 128: Monastery at Debra Labanos dominates the clifftop of one of Ethiopia's many deep gorges.

Photographs by:
Duncan Willetts: pages 1,2/3,4/5,6/7,25,36,37,40,41,44,45,56,57,60,61,64,
65,68,69,72,73,80(below),81,93,96,104,108/9,112,113,119,124/5,126/7,128
Mohamed Amin: pages 76,77,80(top),84,85,88,100/1,122/3,
Santha Faiia: pages 8/9,10/11,20,21,24,28,29,32,48/49,52,53,89,92,97,
105,120/1
John Reader: 16,17